c2

J
598
.33
Sto
	Stone, Lynn M.
	  Puffins / Lynn M. Stone. -- Vero Beach, Fla. :
	Rourke Corp., c1993.
	  24 p. : ill. ; 19 x 20 cm. -- (Unusual animals)
	
	Includes index.
	07306342 LC:93007588 ISBN:0865932816 (lib. bdg.)
	
	1. Puffins. I. Title.

3573   94MAY02   32/06   2-01026788

PUFFINS

UNUSUAL ANIMALS

Lynn M. Stone

The Rourke Corporation, Inc.
Vero Beach, Florida 32964

Edited by Sandra A. Robinson

PHOTO CREDITS
© Lynn M. Stone: title page, pages 4, 7, 13, 15, 18, 21;
© Breck Kent: cover, 17; © Tom Ulrich: pages 8, 10, 12.

Library of Congress Cataloging-in-Publication Data

Stone, Lynn M.
    Puffins / by Lynn M. Stone.
    p.   cm. — (Unusual animals)
    Includes index.
    Summary: Discusses the physical characteristics, homes, and
behavior of these small black and white, flying seabirds.
    ISBN 0-86593-281-6
    1. Puffins—Juvenile literature. [1. Puffins.] I. Title. II. Series:
Stone, Lynn M. Unusual animals.
QL696.C42S86   1993
598.3'3—dc20
                                                        93-7588
                                                           CIP
                                                            AC

TABLE OF CONTENTS

THE UNUSUAL PUFFINS

Puffins are plump, little birds of the northern seas and coasts. With their big, brightly colored heads and beaks, puffins are sometimes mistaken for parrots. With their black and white bodies and love of the sea, puffins are also sometimes mistaken for penguins.

Puffins are amazing birds. For example, they "fly" under water. On land, puffins live like groundhogs—in underground burrows that they dig with their beaks!

Brightly colored beaks earned puffins the nickname of "sea parrots"

THE PUFFINS' COUSINS

Ornithologists are the scientists who study birds. They call the three **species,** or kinds, of puffins and their cousins **alcids,** or auks. Auks are diving birds of the northern oceans.

Auks are not well-known to most people. They have unusual names—dovekies, razorbills, murres, murrelets, auklets and puffins.

Auks live at sea part of the year, far from land. They return to land to nest on rugged, seaside cliffs.

Atlantic puffins share a rock with their cousins, razorbill auks

WHERE PUFFINS LIVE

Small groups of Atlantic puffins live on a few islands off the coast of Maine. More puffins live along the Atlantic coasts of Canada, Greenland, Iceland and several European countries.

The horned puffin has a world-wide population of about 30 million. It lives on Pacific coasts from southern Alaska northward.

The tufted puffin lives on Alaskan islands and along the coasts of Russia and Japan.

Tufted puffins perch on a high cliff in Alaska

HOW PUFFINS LOOK

Each spring, as the nesting season begins, puffins' bodies start to "show off." Their bills become larger and very colorful. The Atlantic puffin's bill becomes red, bluish-gray and ivory. Its webbed feet and eye rings redden.

Tufted puffins develop long, showy feathers that hang from the backs of their heads. All of these changes help the birds attract mates.

By winter, the nesting season is over, and puffins have lost their bright trim. Their bills return to normal size.

A tufted puffin shows off its summer headdress

Horned puffins live along the coasts of North Pacific Ocean

A puffin hunter's shack dots a grassy cliff on an island off Iceland

PUFFIN NESTS

An adult puffin spends much of its life at sea, as far as 500 miles away from land! Each summer, however, it nests in a burrow on a seaside cliff.

Many puffins nest together in the same area, forming a **colony.**

Their many tunnels in the soft earth leave hillsides looking like honeycombs. Puffins dig with their feet and beaks. With great effort, a puffin can move a rock twice the bird's weight.

Burrows of Atlantic puffins honeycomb the soil of Iceland's Westmann Islands

BABY PUFFINS

A female puffin lays one egg. She and her mate take turns sitting on the egg to keep it warm. Six weeks after it is laid, the egg hatches. The baby puffin, or chick, remains in the nest for another six weeks.

A young puffin grows up on a diet of fish. The parents catch fish at sea and carry them, hanging from their bills, to the nest.

An Atlantic puffin, beak draped with fish, returns to the nesting colony

PUFFIN HABITS

The puffin's large, bright bill is important because it attracts mates. Male and female puffins rub their bills together during courtship. Ornithologists call this "billing."

A puffin pumps its stubby wings rapidly. It can fly up to 60 miles per hour. More amazingly, a puffin beats its wings to "fly" under water. Those wings can power a dive that is nearly 200 feet deep. A puffin can stay under water for about a minute.

Stubby wings serve the puffin in flight and undersea

PREDATORS AND PREY

Puffins are hunters, or **predators,** when they dive for fish. They catch such little fish as sardines, herring, smelt and capelin. They also catch other kinds of small **marine,** or sea, creatures.

Amazingly, puffins can catch and carry several fish at one time between their upper and lower bills.

Puffins become **prey** when they are caught by other, larger animals—falcons, eagles, killer whales, river otters and other predators.

Bald eagles spice their diets with puffins

PUFFINS AND PEOPLE

In some places, puffins are caught by hunters who use long-handled nets. The birds are sold for food. In Iceland, smoked puffins are a special treat.

The total puffin population is still large, even though they are hunted by people. Pollution, however, is a real threat to puffins and other sea animals.

In England, rats that escaped from ships have destroyed several puffin colonies.

Glossary

alcid (AL sid) — any one of a group of black and white, flying seabirds that dive for food; puffins, murres, auks and their relatives

colony (KAHL uh nee) — a group of nesting animals of the same kind

marine (muh REEN) — of or relating to the sea, salt water

ornithologist (orn uh THAHL uh jist) — a scientist who studies birds

predator (PRED uh tor) — an animal that kills other animals for food

prey (PRAY) — an animal that is hunted for food by another animal

species (SPEE sheez) — within a group of closely-related animals, such as puffins, one certain kind or type (*Atlantic* puffin)

INDEX